Teacher Created Resources

Read • Think • Do

MATH

Ages 4 & Up

Measuring
Book 1

Ann Montague-Smith

Teacher Created Resources

First published in the United States by
QEB Publishing, Inc.
23062 La Cadena Drive
Laguna Hills
CA 92653

This edition published by
Teacher Created Resources, Inc.
6421 Industry Way
Westminster, CA 92683

www.teachercreated.com

Library of Congress Control Number: 2004102069

ISBN 1-4206-8167-2

Written by Ann Montague-Smith
Designed and edited by The Complete Works
Illustrated by Jenny Tulip
Photography by Steve Lumb and Michael Wicks

Creative Director Louise Morley
Editorial Manager Jean Coppendale

Printed and bound in China

With thanks to:

Contents

Big and little 4

Long, short, wide, and narrow 6

High and low 8

Longer and shorter 10

Heavy and light 12

Heavier and lighter 14

Full and empty 16

Which holds more? 18

I know about the words… 20

Supporting notes for adults 22

Suggestions for using this book 24

Big and little

Point to the big bears.

Now point to the little bears.

Challenge

Find some bears of different sizes. Which bears are big? Which bears are little? Now choose 2 of your bears. Which bear is bigger? Which bear is smaller?

Long, short, wide, and narrow

Which are the long dogs?

Which are the short dogs?

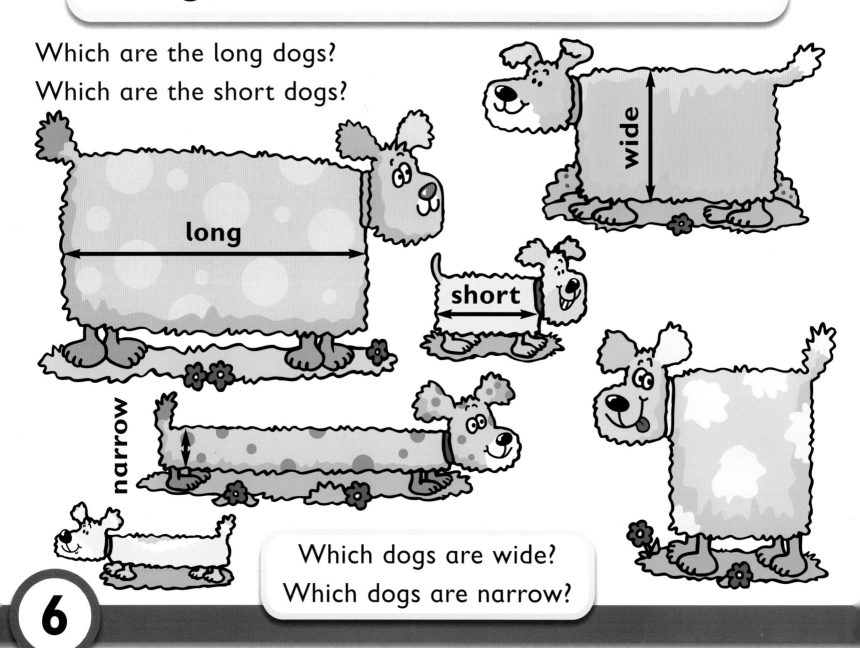

long

wide

short

narrow

Which dogs are wide?

Which dogs are narrow?

Challenge

Find a long and wide dog.
Now look for a dog which
is long and narrow.
Which dogs are short
and wide?

High and low

What can you see high up?

What can you see low down?

8

Challenge

Look around the room you are in. Find 2 things which are high up. Now find 2 things which are low down.

Longer and shorter

Which worms are longer than Wiggly Worm?

WIGGLY WORM

Which worms are shorter than Wiggly Worm?

Challenge
Get some play dough.
Make a worm. Make another
one that is longer. Now make
a worm that is shorter.
Can you put the worms in
order of length?
Start with the shortest worm.

Heavy and light

Which animals are heavy?

Which animals are light?

Challenge

Choose some things in the room you are in. Group the heavy things. Then group the light things.

Heavier and lighter

Point to the heavier toy.

Which toy is lighter?

Challenge

Do this with a friend. Choose 2 toys. Decide which toy is heavier by holding them. Now check by putting the toys onto a balance.

Full and empty

Point to the bottles which are full.

Now point to the bottles which are not full.
Which ones are empty?

16

Challenge

Get some dry sand.
Find some things to fill.
Fill them up.
Empty them out.
Now make them half full.

Which holds more?

Point to the one in each set that holds more.

Now point to the one that holds less.

18

Challenge

Get some dry sand and 2 different pots. By pouring sand, find out which pot holds more. So which pot holds less?

I know about the words...

Get some board game tokens.

Listen to the words.

Put a token on the picture that matches.

holds more

holds less

little

big

wide

wider

narrow

narrower

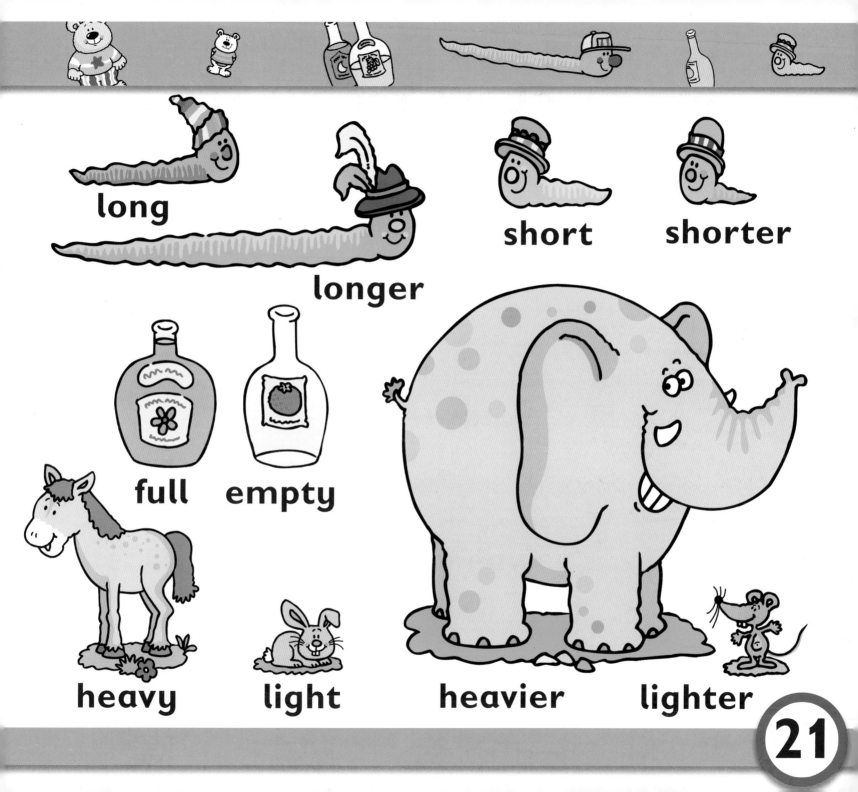

long

longer

short

shorter

full

empty

heavy

light

heavier

lighter

21

Supporting notes for adults

Big and little – pages 4-5

Talk about the bears on the page. Encourage the children to decide
which is "big" and which is "little" in each pair. Ask, "Why do you think so?"

Long, short, wide, and narrow – pages 6-7

The children may not agree on which is long/short/wide/narrow.
Encourage them to explain why they made their choices.

High and low – pages 8-9

If the children are unsure of "high" and "low," encourage them to stretch up high, then
bend down low as you say these words. Then ask them to touch something high up in
the room, such as a point as high up the wall as they can reach, then low down, such as the floor.

Longer and shorter – pages 10-11

If children find making comparisons of length difficult, show them how to put a
piece of string along Wiggly Worm, then cut the string to Wiggly's length.
Now they can use the string to compare the lengths of the other worms.

Heavy and light – pages 12-13

If the children are unsure about the vocabulary, put out some items for the children to hold. Ask, "Is this heavy? Which one is light?"

Heavier and lighter – pages 14-15

If the children are unsure about which side of the balance shows "heavier" and which shows "lighter," use a balance with some toys. Talk about how the heavier side moves "down" and the lighter side "up." Challenge the children to say what would happen if the 2 toys were about the same weight, then demonstrate this with 2 identical toys.

Full and empty – pages 16-17

If the children are unsure about the vocabulary, demonstrate "full," "empty," and "is part full" using sand or water and some containers.

Which holds more? – pages 18-19

If children do not understand about holding more and less, use some dry sand or water and some containers. Give the children time to pour from one container to the other. Ask, "Did all the sand fit? So which one holds more/less?"

I know about the words… – pages 20-21

Read the words under each picture. Ask the children to say which picture shows that word. Some of the pictures will have 2 ideas, such as "heavier" and "lighter." Encourage the children to show you which part of the picture depicts each idea.

I know about the words… – pages 20-21
Which holds more? – pages 18-19

Suggestions for using this book

Children will enjoy looking through the book and talking about the colorful pictures. Sit somewhere comfortable together. Read the instructions to the children, then encourage them to take part in the activity and check whether or not they understand what to do.

When comparing two things for length, ask, "Which is longer or shorter… wider or narrower?" for each pair. Check that the children are making a direct comparison. They will need to make sure that both objects are level, so placing them on a table, or side by side, will help.

The images in the book can be used as starting points, so that the children go away to try some comparing of lengths, weights, or capacities. Always encourage them to guess first, so that they are making an estimate. Then they can make comparisons to check if they made a good guess. Estimating skills improve with practice and through checking by measuring.

If there is no balance handy for the children to make comparisons of weight, they could use an ordinary household scale, but they will need some help in interpreting this. It is easier for the children to see what is happening if a balance-type scale can be used.

In capacity, where children are filling and pouring from containers, they may need to be reminded that in everyday life we do not fill things to the brim. Encourage them to talk about what would happen if we tried to drink from a cup that was full to the brim. However, when filling and pouring, and especially when using dry sand, children will want to fill containers up to the brim.